*Other titles
by
Corey Hamilton*

**Keep Left
Society's Grip
Exit Is A Safe Place
No One Shall Be Spared
Mash Notes
Mash Notes: vol 2
Too Personal
Lonely Night Songs
2 Days
Unhyped
Time Marches On
Thirty Three
VI
What If?
Magic Bus
How I Remember It
Cease & Desist
Sensible Shoes
Do Not Ever Have Any Good Ideas
DNA
I Am NOT With The Band
Wedges Politics
My Side Project**

opEN uP

Copyright © 2005 Corey Hamilton

All rights reserved. No part of this book may be reproduced or transmitted in any form or by any means, graphic, mechanical or electronic, including photocopying and recording, or by any information storage or retrieval system without written permission from the publisher, except for brief passages quoted in review.

Library and Archives Canada Cataloguing in Publication

Hamilton, Coery, 1971-
    Open up / Corey Hamilton.

Poems.
ISBN 978-0-9697305-2-1

    I. Title.

PS8565.A5347O64 2008   C811'.54   C2007-906818-9

Front cover painting and back cover photograph © 2004 Corey Hamilton
Design/Layout by Corey Hamilton

First Printing

Published by Dramatic Situations
       P.O. Box 696
       Edmonton, AB
       T5J 2L4
       CANADA
www.dramaticsituations.com

printed on 100% recycled paper.

opEN uP

corEY hamiLtON

f.Y.I.

i haVE bEEn nUMbERinG My wRItiNGs/PIecES sINce HiGH SChOOl. ThIS iS mY fIrST bOok thAt is (1)cOMPLetely POeTRy aNd (2)IN nuMerICal ORdER. ThaT, iS,I gRAbbED a BunCH Of pIEceS iN oRDER aND mAde a BoOk. "OPen up" iS mIssInG oNE PIEcE, #1265. iT iS iN"n0 oNE sHAlL bE sPaReD". ALSo, I TRiED t0 wRIte OnE poEM a DAy fOR ovEr a mOnth. foR tHE mOSt pART iT wORkED. #1247-1294 aRE thESe piECEs. On oNE daY i wrotE noTHing, tHE daY aFTer I wrOTE tWo piEces. therE waS aNOthER daY i wRotE tWo piecES aND thEN on AnothER daY i wroTE thREe.

i aM vERy haPPY wITh THis bOOk, i hOPe thaT yOU eNJoy tHe reaD.

thANks.

THE BEGINNING OF A NEW BOOK

Shadows of ideas
Are reflections of light
Channeled the right way
Are sharper than a razor
Or even a bee's stinger
They are chain links
Of a million independents
That you could support
And that you would
Go to the firing squad for
We are all filled
With joy and pain
To a certain degree
Channel each
And you have electricity
Pure power
Don't re-write and
You have raw power
Enough to heat an arctic city
For years to come
Giving hope to all of its' civilians
For years to come

WITHOUT ME

I've never been found like this before
Does it all,
The whole package,
Surprise you?
Are you taken aback?
HEY!
I'll ask the questions
And you give me the answers promptly
And about your opinion
If I want one
I'll give you one
Because I am the prize
At the bottom of the box
You are the finder
And there is a finder's fee
And it is deposited
Directly into my retirement plan
All relationships end
Sooner or later
But I get paid for my services
Or it's your knee caps
On my mantlepiece
Now that I have been found
If I am not what you expected
Good
If I am what you expected
That's good too
Because
It will be the same without you
But it will never be the same
Without me

ON YOUR ASS

There is no fire in your eyes
There is a full belly of alcohol though
And your boyfriend's hand
On your ass
I want to stop the world
From turning
To pit you against an eternal darkness
To see if you would implode
You would kick my ass at chess
But I am driven enough to know
That your youth
Is my burden
And that last meeting
Where I was so cold
Was inevitable
Because of your ignorance
In not returning my calls
Was it a waste of time even calling you?
Yes
Because your youth
Is my burden
And I am driven enough to know
A raw deal
And a good one
Your inactions are the raw one
My drive the good
By the way
I can't look at my semi-lonely life
As a raw or good deal
It just has to be
In order for my drive
And the fire in _my_ eyes
To continue
Pray

That we don't meet again
For if we do
I will knock you
On the same place
Where your boyfriend's hand is

MY GOALS

My goals
Don't need to travel
My ambition
Is pretty
Stationary
Right now
But that's O.K.
Everything in its own time

My goals
Keep me travelling
On the inside
So tight
Like my drive
Which will take me
Higher
Than most

My goals
Have a home
With me
And way on
The internet
With all of the wannabees
That will never be
But my breathing never stops

Their's will
Unlike my will
Unlike my ambition
Unlike my drive
You don't need to step on others
But you have to be
Firm like

My goals

Eventually
It will all come together
And when it does
You won't know
What hit you
Because I will act
Like I've been there all along
With my goals

I have been there all along
You just never noticed
Because you had
Your blinders on
Because my drive
Is as bright as
My goals
Nothing like it before
Nothing like it again

My goals

#1199

One doubt
And you'll lose
Your place to live
To doubt constantly
And you'll lose
Everything

LIKE NEIL SAID

I've never had the feeling
That "Tonight's The Night"
Like Neil said
I've led a fairly clean life
But I have known
A few people
To disappear
Only to find out later
That they are now buried
That was their problem
The moment that they left my life
I stopped worrying about them
And forgot about
Forgetting to go to that concert
I could hardly wait for
Oh well
Snooze
You lose
It's how I feel
From day to day
Because the music is so loud
I can't write
But that's O.K.
I will move on
I may fall off of the horse
But hopefully
The future holds steady
And I am strong enough
To get back on
Again and again
I thought that I met you
Thirteen years ago
On a cold night
In a cold hall

Where a couple of bands
I liked were playing
I was at the merch table
And fuck was I lonely
You came up and told me
Your name and
Talked to me like I was a friend
You were waiting
To use the washroom
And I was waiting
For someone different
Your name was different
So different
I wrote about it
And even though I forgot the poem
I remembered your name
And I had another crush again
Now
I am a lot older and fatter
And I run into you
I will ask if it was you
You are still beautiful
With your unique name
And a voice
That gets me acting like a school boy
And hoping that
This old record
Doesn't skip
And holds out a little while longer
If it was you
And is you
We'll see what happens
Even if you pop out
Of my life again
What you brought out of me
Means more to me
Than what the
Six feet under group

Ever did
But I guess you and the group
Both made me spill
Onto paper
The only difference is
That the six feet under group
Has no hope
And you
With your different name and style
Have hope
That brings me out of the cold
And believe in fiction like love

LOSE TO WIN

You have to lose
To learn how to win
Eventually
You will fly
And I will be a witness
To your losses
And then
All your glory
As I hope
You will with me

You can't win
If you don't play
By the same token
You can't play
If you don't win
You can't be afraid
To lose everything
Or gain nothing
Just make it instinctual
And blow yourself away

As I hope
You will with me
As I hope

#1202

NEVER GOING TO GET IT

It's just outside of your
Back door
It's just out of reach of your
Grasping paws
It's a few miles an hour faster
Than you are
It's just me
My meaning
And my work's meaning
And that's how
I will keep it
Because if you don't get it
By now
Then you are never going to

ICE CREAM MAN

I don't trust you
The sound of the ice cream man
It just makes me blush
And get embarrassed
Because I never once
Bought anything from one
It's just the jingly music
Makes me want to be
A child again
Hoping that he will have
Something for me
To cure my awkwardness
Of my child years
The sound of the music
Makes me feel vulnerable
I guess that's why I blush
And get embarrassed
I don't want to remember
My youth
Twenty or so years is a long time
But it can't do anything
For the betrayal of
My youth
By other youth
Vulnerability
Maybe the ice cream man
Feels this too
For he has no protection
From robbery or such
So he has to go on faith
Faith is in short supply
When you read about
Teenagers forcing a
Mentally challenged boy

To lick a dirty toilet bowl

I hear the music
And I worry about him
And I remember my childhood
Both are reasons why
I get embarrassed
When I hear the ice cream man's music
In the middle of a hot summer

PINCH ME, I MUST BE DREAMING

I just woke up from a dream
In it
My mother was cursing
Some of my personality traits
To my sisters
My sisters leapt to my defense
I was in the other room
Listening to everything
They didn't know this

My mother
Probably has cursed
Some of my personality traits
But my sisters
Have never and
Would never leap to my defense
Not to my mother
Or anyone else
For that matter
These are facts

I trusted them all
To teach me
To never trust anyone but myself
I have also learned that
I am the only one
Who will have to leap to my defense
They don't know me
And never will
What else can I say

I am happy with how things have worked out

IT WILL FOLLOW YOU

Can you escape your own motives?
No
You've dug in too deep
And now you're caught
You're sussed and all
We could never be friends
It was never in the cards
You're laid out in some guy's mansion
And I am still hoping for a win
I am drinking jet fuel
So I can keep up with my ideas
You're on your back
In his bed
With his money in you
I won't renew this book
From the library
I've read it before
The characters are weak
The plot is thin
And it doesn't even have a good cover
Do you ever feel guilty
About leaving our team
And going to his much bigger payroll?
I don't know
And I never will
Unless you turn up in the tabloids
I won't ever see you again
And that suits me just fine
I've been alone most of my life
So what's a little while longer

So how can you sleep at night?

NOW

Your choice
Is to be made now
A decision
Has to be made now
Are you ever going to feel
Like this again
Or will you just pass on by
Again
There is no "yes" or "no"
Answer
There is no right or wrong
Answer
It's just that everything
Must be as clear as a
Cloudless breezeless
Summer night
So
What will it be
To be with me
Or to pass the buck
Make it
Now

FOR ANOTHER

She told me
To enjoy myself
I do
I just wish
That for once
At my day job
Somebody would
I just wish
That for once
(In a long time)
A woman
I was interested in
Would enjoy myself
Instead of asking myself
How my friend feels about herself
When it rains
When it finally rains
It will wash all this crap away
And I will be clean once again
And another rotation of the clock
And it's another scar
Another poem
Another painting
Another photograph
Another poster
Another book
Another record
Another cd
Another another
Another
Another year
We'll see what happens tomorrow
Another "enjoy myself"
And I'll throw up my testicles

And start all over again
Enjoy myself
I know you're closed
But I will remain open
For another day
For another month
For another year
That I carry that lie around
For another second?
Hopefully
Hope
Hopefully

EMOTIONAL RAPIST

What happened to you
After your last drink
And cigarette
You burned down
To the filter
And were left empty
Like your last bottle of beer
You're just a boring mess
Without it
And with it
You are mean
Like a great white shark
Always the predator
Always on the look out
For your next victim
Continue on
And you will end up in jail
Or worse
Dead
Or are you already
Worse
Sign here son of a bitch
Even though you don't understand
The wind blowing down
The avenue
When will you change?
When we tattoo it
on your forehead?
Eventually
We'll drive your kind underground
And we won't need
Alcohol or drugs
Subversive or not
We'll drive you underground

Whether or not
You figure out
What happened to you

#1209

YOU YOUR OWN PROVIDER

Time
Has left you behind
In the dust
You couldn't keep up
So you dropped out
Onto your knees
Gasping for air
You are only 19
But you thought
Getting pregnant
Was the right thing to do
Now you are sick
And can't keep a job
And your apartment
Above the pawn shop
Never gets quiet enough
To get a sleep pattern
I have got a secret to tell you

You made a mistake

You made a mistake
And It's too late to turn back
Or stop it
Because time left your side
So bad
That now a bleak future
Is predetermined
I bet you
That he will leave you
Once the jig is up
And the responsibility
Falls into place
How do you end this

When it started so innocently
You can't stop
A freight train
With a bag of marshmallows
Admit it

You made a mistake

And you need a hand
From someone
Who won't say "I told you so"
I wonder about your friends
And your family
If they all told you so
I can't help you much
Because I am just going by rumors
And I am not a parent
And I am not friend
And I am not family
I am an innocent bystander
Who has kept out of trouble
For the most part
And I just hope that you find
A provider in yourself
To move on from
Your mistake

TRUST YOU

Celine said that
Trust takes the place of love
In frightened people
I am frightened
And I trust you
To show me some new rules
For me to break
And to impress you
Trust you
To hurt me
When it's for the best
The best for both of us
Trust me
To show you
What I am capable of
Capable of greatness in me
Trust me
Not to let you down
In your time of need
Because you were there
Always for me
Is it bad to trust before love?
No
Is it good to replace love for trust
Just because you are frightened?
No
Trust then love
Don't be frightened of either

TABLE IN THE BACK

Someday
When my words don't fade away
So easily
And are remembered fondly
Like a lover's caress
Or a baby's giggle
I will arrive at a place
Where I won't be shunned
And I will be greeted
With open hearts, minds and arms
I will have my own table
In the back
Where everyone will have to pass
To go see the view
Of the river valley
I know it's a funny place
For the back to be
For the view to be
But it's just perfect for me
It's an odd place for everything
But it's just right for me
Someday
Here
Will be remembered
Thoughtfully respected
For all my words of passion
My passion doesn't keep
The roof above my head
But it keeps my head above all else
And someday
When my words don't fade away
So viciously, easily
They will keep the roof
Above my head

My passion will keep the roof
Above my head
As well as keeping
My head above all else
Contradictions abound
I will live off these words
Sitting at the table in the back
On the occasional night out
And will be at peace
With my words, head and heart
And your open hearts, minds and arms
I will be at peace
With myself and my words
At the table in the back
What better story could there be?
Than having your words
Remembered fondly
And having your own
Table in the back
And knowing full well
That you can finish your meal
And return to your home
That your words of passion paid for

IN GOOD TIME

Treat me as unkind as you want
It will come back to haunt you
In good time
Give up everything for free
Makes sure nothing goes to me
Eventually
You will have to bend over
To take it for a long time
You're only 21 and that's fine
Grow up a little more
Lose the jealous boyfriend
And maybe my opinion will change
But if you don't
My opinion won't
Not for a long time
And that's fine with me
What goes around
Comes around
All in good time

POSITIVE MUTE

I wash my hands
I wash my face
I wash my body
And try to cleanse myself
Of these nightmares and
Bad thoughts
I must not think
Bad thoughts
I must become
A more positive mute
Concentrate more
On making,
On forcing my work
To be more positive
As a reflection of myself trying
To be more positive
And let my work
Do all the talking
And cleanse my body
From the negative
Let the positive shine through
My clean talking work
My clean talking body
My clean talking body of work

BACK POCKET HOPE

I've got hope
In my back pocket
And on the back of my neck
It is better in my back pocket
Because I can pull it out
At my leisure
The back of my neck
Is for my followers
Twist around
And maybe I will see hope
On my neck
In my bathroom mirror
Someone told me
That it's not supposed to be there
But I don't care
It helps me get through
When my back pocket
Gets a hole in it
And I lose the hope in it
You should always have back up
Always always always
And I have got my back up
My back pocket
And the back of my neck
They both keep me going
When I am low

COIN FOR PAIN

The hands are clapping
And they are clapping for you
I sat in your shadow
In a train
That had stopped dead in its' tracks
I had no problem with
The cling-ons that surrounded
You and I
Oh well
Life is never perfect
Least of all
For me
I write it all down
To pass it off as a diary
A public/private diary
In the hopes
Of making some coin
Off of my discomfort
I mean why not?
Why shouldn't I?
I was never jealous
Of your friends clapping hands
I was envious
Fuck
Now I am splitting hairs
In a few days
I'll send you an e-mail
And hope that you respond
So the dialogue continues
And I can say
"You get coin for your discomfort"
And then I'll ask
"Why not me?"

AND SHOUT

I poke it

Just to see how much it hurts

I am wearing a shirt that says

"You are dreaming of me"

You would pay for shit like that

For me

It is free

It comes to me for free

Now I poke you

Just to see how much it bothers you

Now you are wearing a shirt that says

"Whisper in my ear"

You paid for that shit

And for you

I put a bullhorn to your ear

And shout

PESSIMISTIC METEOROLOGIST

You are my witness
To my crime
Of not saving for a rainy day
Of not being patient
"Don't let me die young"
I used to say
Now I am not so sure
It has been raining for years
And according to your forecast
It won't end soon
You are the birth of my pessimism
You are the death of my optimism
I have to be the birth of my realism
One day this rain is going to end
And when it does
You'll be sorry
That you ever predicted
Such a bleak future for me
When eventually
I will turn around
And be your witness
To your crimes
Against me

TENDER HOURS

Listen
You can hear me
Not coming home tonight
It is a small request
For you
Not to hesitate
In the tender hours
You <u>will</u> miss me
You know it
And I know it too
But I won't make fun of you
For missing me
Everyone has to miss someone
In the tender hours
Listen
In the distance
You can hear me yell
"BINGO!"
Even though I don't play bingo
That's the thought
That will stay with me
For a long time
Will it be a thought
For you to remember
Or will missing me
Be enough?
Remember
No hesitating
First words
From the back of your brain
And out of your mouth

Missing you
Missing me

In the tender hours
In the tender hours

#1220

WHO ARE YOU ANYWAYS?

When I win tomorrow
Will you jump on my bandwagon
Then
Or will you still get up and get out
At the sound of my voice
Away
Unlike the few who
Have been around me
With
Enough of a push
To keep me going
You
Are too small for me to worry about
From tomorrow on
So
Then
Away
With
You

TOMORROW

I have written about

Tomorrow

In a positive manner

Very cocky sometimes too

Other times

With indifference

And sometimes with the dread

Of someone who is going to be

Executed at dawn

Tomorrow

But a glorious beginning

For a new bright

Tomorrow

Seems just out of reach

And all of my

Dreams and hopes

Are dashed

When I awake at dawn

When my body goes through

All the motions

And again

I've written about

Tomorrow

Which never seems

To live up to my expectations

Tomorrow

Are you just a movie

Or someone else's reality?

If so

When will you be

My tomorrow?

UNDERDOG WINS

Who would have thought
I would have all this stuff
To keep me going
Through the heat and the cold
Through the night and the day
Until I finally win the prize
The prize that suits me the most
My hand writing changes
With every word
Until someone puts up with it
And subjects me to some more
Of my guilty praise
And it finally turns risk to reward
To demand to sells
And to my paycheque
I am not looking for answers
I have got them all in my note books
And on my body
Who would have thought
I wouldn't burn another bridge
And I am finally rewarded
With respect and a paycheque

#1223

PUBLISHERS

You can't see with your ears
You can't hear with your mouth
You can't taste with your nose
And you can't smell with your fingers
But you can hear the rules of this game
Loud and clear
You can taste your own blood
And smell your own fear
Even though you are just out of reach
The rules say it's too much
And then they hit you hard in the face
For your honesty crime
Normally this would be bearable
But on a day like today
It is just too much
To just shrug it off
Because so much
Time and effort and money
Blood and sweat and tears
Went into it
That now you have to start over
And even though
This all builds character
It eats you up
By folding up
And hearing
"NO."
Again

#1224

If you get something for free
Then it's not worth holding onto
So do your best to give it away
And make someone else's life special too

#1225

NEVER

Nothing is forgotten around her
Because I fall apart
On a regular basis
I don't feel so strong
Right now
Maybe they can give me another pill
For that
I know
Deep down inside
I know
I will never see them again
And that is fine with me
A few less plastic people
In my life
The better
I gave it my best shot
To like them
But they reminded me
Too much of my sisters
With their
Houses
And cars
And pets
And spouses
And
And
And
I will never feel
Comfortable around them
Nothing is forgotten around me
Because I keep on getting on up
When they least expect it
I hate you all
For making me write this

I hate you all
For your banter I hear
When we are all together
You make me want to disappear
And again I will reiterate
I hate you all
I hate you all
For making me write this

TRIGGER HAPPY

What do you hear
When you and I talk
Do you hear a desperate man
Do you hear a sad man
Do you hear an angry man
Or do you hear at all
I had a dream last night
That I lost all of my extra weight
And my tattoos faded away
And I shaved off my beard
And let the hair on my head
Grow out to a respectable length
I cleaned myself up
And they took away all of my pills
Because they felt that
I didn't need them anymore
Because I smiled more often than not
But
In a little while
I just got sad again
And never left my apartment
I put up black curtains
And painted over my mirrors
And never ventured far
Except for groceries
I never saw anyone again
Except for the person
That I bought the gun from
Then I went home
Put the gun to my head
And pulled the trigger
Did you hear
Whenever we talked?
You didn't seem to care

So I went so far
I couldn't get back

Now what do you hear?

EVEN QUICKER

Your car rolled quickly into the ocean
And started filling up with water
Even quicker
You couldn't get your seatbelts undone
And the car was filling with water
So fast that you couldn't get out
Quick enough
So you drowned
The car settled on the bottom
Of the ocean
And you disappeared into your watery grave
We will never see you again
Now
Your car is a home
To all sorts of underwater wildlife
And we'll never see you again
And after awhile
We won't miss you either

DIE ALONE

Now
I will tell you why
People die alone
I saw you yesterday
You didn't recognize me
Fifteen years ago
We were friends
But I've gained weight
Tattoos, different glasses
And a beard
You were the same
You still had that
Youthful nervous look about you
Like you were waiting
For someone's foot
To kick your ass
I was going to say "hi."
But thought better of it
When I moved out of the suburbs
That many years ago
You never called me again
So why bother
Trying to re-attach to something
That is long gone
This is why people like me
Die alone

#1229

Hope is an ungracious tool
When everything goes perfectly
When everything goes off just as planned
But hope is a lifeline
When nothing goes right
And you are left crying alone
In your bed at night

TWO EX-COWORKERS

You are nothing more
Than a high school power tripping bully to me

In grade ten phys ed class
At the end of day one, class one
I walked into the boy's change room
And was greeted with a fist
To my nose
Bleeding
I buckled
And was put in a headlock
My head was repeatedly
Smashed into locker doors
As I noticed my blood
Dripping on the ground
As I was losing consciousness
I remembered the nerve clusters
In one's neck
And I grabbed them with my left hand
And crushed them
He released me immediately
And I fell to the floor

Moments later
We were hauled into
The teacher's office
And yelled at
And then made to shake hands
I have always regretted
Shaking your hand
The next day
You came to phys ed class
In a neck brace
Complaining to me

About the pain you were in
Not even considering
My nose, head
Or my pride
When you verbally harassed me
All class
Before you punched me
In the nose

You are nothing more
Than a high school power tripping bully to me
That cost me my job
The other day
If we meet again
I will ignore you
But smile
Knowing that
One day
When you are extremely snotty
And pulling the power trip
Someone will shit
On the hood of your car
And you will wonder
What brought this on
And why it had to happen to you
And I will be around the corner
Watching it all
Laughing at the whole situation
What goes around
Comes around
Maybe not from me
But someone else will
Stand on your feet
And I will be around the corner
Watching it all
Laughing at the whole situation
Because
What goes around

Comes around
And it can't happen
To a more worthy person
Than you
The high school power tripping bully

YOUR PROCTOLOGIST CALLED

"Hands off buddy!"
She said with an irritated tone
After I poked her
In the ribs
"Yes dear."
I responded sarcastically
Had it been the guy to my right
Or maybe Brad Pitt or Denzel Washington
Or if she swings the other way
Nicole Kidman or Janet Jackson
She probably wouldn't minded
One bit

You know the type
The girls/women
Who wear virtually nothing
And unless you are Tom Cruise
Or Sandra Bullock
(If she swings that way)
Are the only one who should look
But when a 32 year old
Bald, fat guy covered in tattoos
Like,
Me for instance
Looks at her
There is a scowl and then she huffs
And scurries away
Basically saying
That she didn't want me looking
Just the Tom Cruise/Sandra Bullock type
Who are good looking
<u>And</u> wealthy
Looking at her

If you don't want me
(And the rest of the world looking
For that fact)
Then put some clothes on
SNOB
If you don't want me touching
(And the rest of the world touching
For that fact)
Then don't let anyone else touch
And don't go touching anyone
HYPOCRITE

My 60 year old male friend would say
"Cock tease,
Not worth their weight in shit."
My Dad would say
Those who talked about sex a lot
(Like the one I poked)
Aren't getting any
Those who are having sex
Don't need to brag
And/or talk about it

So if you don't want to be
The center of everyone's attention
Then put some fucking clothes on
And shut your fucking yap
The only good thing about running into
Girls/women like this is
It is more ammunition for my next book

Oh,
Lady,
By the way,
Your proctologist called,
They found your head.

FORGET TO LIVE

I forgot you
The moment after I hung up
On you
And I remember
That Borges said that
We all live by leaving behind
So I left you behind
In the dust
It it's the healthiest way
To move on
And
No
I won't stalk you
Because that is a waste of energy
Energy that would be
Better suited for my work
Which is more important
Than anything else
In or out of my life
My work keeps me going
A scorned woman doesn't
I forgot you
In order to live
And with my work
I will never forget to live

PROMISES ARE JUST WORDS

Hollow and empty
From reading some promises
Sorry
Just reading words
You don't know what it's like in here
With all of the visitors
And all of the people
Who think that they are my boss
When I don't have one
Except myself
Myself as a boss
I think that I would make a pretty good one
I mean....
I've read lots about being a boss
Kafka, Camus, Celine, Borges, etc., etc., etc.
So again,
I think I would make a good boss
One hundred years ago
I decided to exterminate
Everyone around me
So I did
I don't regret it one iota
I made sure that they all died horribly
To be honest
I made a promise
And I kept it
And now you expect me
To go back on my "just words"
Or my promise and make it
"Just words"
Go to hell if you believe in it
I get to sleep just fine
And you?
You never kept one promise to me

You threw out "just words"
And I was fished in
Hook, line and sinker
That's why I exterminated you
Everyone of you
I kept pouring liquid Draino
Into your breakfast cereal
Until it ate your guts
(What little guts you had)
And you died
Then I took 3 months off
From being an artist, worker, whatever
And cut up your bodies
Into bite sized morsels
And scattered them around the globe
Got home and retired
I then decided that
I wouldn't be a good boss
Of "others"
Because "others"
Never keep their promises
And I do
So now I am my own boss
And loving it
Just remember....
If you want me as your boss
And you break your promise
Or just give out just words
And it's another hundred years for me
And for you....
Please....
Let's not go there

#1234

JUST TO MAKE SURE

It has been said before
And I will say it again
Because I have got nothing to lose
And I just realized
I have everything to gain
So
If you are going to break me
You had better kill me
Because if you don't
I will find out where you sleep
And set you on fire
And knock the shit out of you
With an aluminum bat
Just to make sure that you die

Just to make sure
I said I love you again
Just before you hung up on me
Then I knew that you didn't care
So I found out where I slept
And set myself on fire
All the while I let your better looking sister
Knock the shit out of me
With an aluminum bat
And that is when I knew
You couldn't care less about me
But I had to make sure
So I died that evening
Just to make sure

Yesterday I went out
And bought the farm
And instead of planting crops
I planted lots of trees

And claymore mines
Just for the hunters and trespassers
I built an environmentally friendly house
Bought a hybrid car
And I sat in the car
Listening to Slayer
At an ear bleed volume
While the car sat running in the closed garage
With a pipe
From you know where to you know how
I could still hear the explosions
So I went to sleep
Just to make sure
I wouldn't hear anymore explosions
After that I paid your better looking sister
Enough to cover the both of you
To burn down my house
With all of my work in it
And as a surprise
I left a note
For the hunters and trespassers
Explaining that the two of you
Were responsible for everything

So they hunted the two of you down
And skinned you alive
All the while calling you white supremist shit
And then the whole damn thing collapsed
In on everybody
And that was done just to make sure
No one got out alive

Just to make sure
No one got out alive

#1235

COMES AND GOES

I just got home
From my volunteer job
Slightly cold and wet
From the cold rain
That patted me on
My coatless body
So I thought I would do some writing
About a young woman I met
Three or four shifts ago
And was in again this evening

I volunteer at a small art gallery
In a hospital
So lots of patients
Come and go
One evening
Three or four shifts ago
A young woman
With a pretty face
And long blonde hair
Came in
In a wheel chair
To look at the art
I briefly stopped reading
To greet her generically
As she slowly wheeled herself in
I continued reading
After awhile I noticed her
At the guest book
For quite awhile
I watched her intently
Partially because of her beauty
And partially because some of the patients
Had written some pretty derogatory words

In the past
That we've had
To apply heavy layers of liquid paper to
When she looked up
I could tell
That she wasn't one of them
Because her eyes were bright and shiny
She asked me
What I thought of the current exhibition
And I told her
And after that we talked
Because she had broken the ice
As it were
I told her that I painted as well
She said that she had tried it today
In water colors
And she wanted to show them to me
But before she wheeled herself away
She said her name was Karen
And that she could walk
So she didn't need the wheelchair
But she needed the exercise
Then Karen asked me
If I liked what I did in the gallery
I said that for the most part
Yes I did
And that I would scratch her off
As being a patient
Karen said she was a patient
And showed me her wrist band
That was carefully hidden underneath
Her long sleeved shirt
I never asked her
What she was in for
We are told never to ask that
We chatted a little more
Before she wheeled herself away
To get her painting to show me

Fifteen minutes later
She was back
With a simple water colour painting
Of trees, sky and earth
Karen was embarrassed
At how simple it was
But I told her
We all start out simple
And that we all just need practice
She asked for my advice
I gave her what tips I could
Because I rarely painted in water colors
Mostly oils and acrylics
Because if you make a mistake
In water colors
You might as well throw it out
For you can't hide your mistakes all that well
Like you can hide them in oils and acrylics
This is some of what I told her
Next Karen showed me a sculpture
She had created out of scraps of tiles
Which I genuinely thought and felt was brilliant
We chatted about this and that
And then we said our goodnights
And she wheeled herself back to her ward
I thought to myself
That I would never see Karen again

Two shifts later
I saw her shoulder to shoulder
With an angry young man
Who had a scowl on his face
So I pretended not to see
Karen and her "boyfriend"
Seconds later there was tapping
Tap tapping on the glass
And it was Karen's young face smiling

While she waved
While I waved
Her "boyfriend" glared at me
I just continued to wave
And they came and went
And that was that

Sometimes I jump to conclusions
But I hate it when
The female friends I have
Have jealous boyfriends
Who insist on making me
Feel like an alien
If I had a loonie
For everytime some shithead guy said
"Hey, you tryin' to pick up my girl?"
I would be
Donald Trump's renter/roommate
Ahhhh
I can see it now
Gold plated bathroom sinks
And mirrors everywhere
When I look back at Karen's "boyfriend"
Giving me the evil eye
It's like, look buddy
Lose the jealousy
Because as I get older
I have noticed that
The urge for a lover is dwindling
And my urge to do my work
Is growing tenfold
So as for me wanting
To bump uglies with "your girl"
It just wasn't there
What was there
Was a worry
A worry that always comes
A worry that the guy

Is going to hit or yell
Or hit and yell
Because of me
I worry because the jealousy
I see
Is almost always in young men
I have never seen it in a 40 year old
Who has been married 20 years
It's always angry young men
It's always angry drunk young men
It always angry stoned young men
Or middle aged stalkers
Who haven't learned
To grow out of an angry young man
I have seen all of these
Angry young men
On the avenue
Fighting and/or puking
They all see me as a threat
Which I don't understand
Because I sure as hell ain't no Brad Pitt
In the looks or finances departments
So I will never get it

I think back to the few lovers
I have had and realize
That I was never that way
But I may have been
Had I been a drunk, stoned, angry young man
But I quit drinking and drugging years before
My first girlfriend
I was never the jealous type
Maybe because
My sense of trust and loyalty
Towards my few lovers never faltered
And I never had a substance abuse problem
With my lovers around
To help it falter

So I can't understand it
Maybe because
For the most part
I was able to keep my anger in check
From my judo training
From my judo sensei
Teaching me to channel it
Only in tournaments or
In acts of self defense
Which jealousy falls into neither
Yes, that's it
I was never an angry young man
I was just lonely and friendly

So back to tonight
Karen stopped by
To return some paints and other supplies
She had borrowed from the gallery
When the gallery had a drop it studio the other day
We chatted a bit more
Until she told me that
She was getting discharged tomorrow
And that she would stop by sometime
We shook hands
And I thought
Fuck it
He's nowhere in sight
So I gently kissed her hand
I know I shouldn't have, but....
I couldn't resist
Karen lifted her hand again and said
"I want another one"
And I thought
Fuck it
He's nowhere in sight
And I hope that right now
He is flinching
Because the kisses are

Payback for glaring

And making me worry

Worry that he is abusive

Worry that she was in the psych ward

Worry worry worry worry

I will always worry

That I screwed it up

For a beautiful girl named Karen

Who comes and goes

But I will still be here

But Karen came and went

Worry worry worry

About the girl friends

Who come and go in my life

Most times I never mean to make the men jealous

Because most times

I am just lonely and friendly

#1236

CHUGS

You are always into talking

But you never have anything to say

So nothing is done right

But you can't help someone

Who doesn't want help

So the best thing

To do with people like that

Is to exterminate them

They only want hand outs

So they can go get drunk

So the best thing

To do with people like that

Is to exterminate them

Like the worthless

Cockroaches that they are

The worthless cockroaches

Are always into talking

But they never have anything to say

So nothing is done right

But you can't help

Someone who wants

Your spare change

They don't want your help

They want your bottles and change

They don't want your help

They want your change

Not their change

So the best thing

To do with people like that

Is to exterminate them

Exterminate them all

#1237

DO YOU ENJOY TORTURING ME?

I felt dirty
After I wrote my last piece
So I cut myself
And listened to depressing music
Realizing that no one
Misses me the most
The family is a burden
A burden I can't bear anymore
I am the odd man out
Waiting to see what the night
Will bring
More of the same
More of the same
Will you ever see me
When the sun rises
All the parents around me
Make sure their offspring
Will have it better than they did
Not mine
Whenever I am in dire straits
I get the third degree
I always say "I will pay you back"
And they say
They are not worried about it
I cry out
Why did you put me through the ringer then?!
I have the scars
To prove all of this
Here
I will show them to you
I will always draw blood
It's best this way
Because there is no other way
This cleanses me

Because I feel dirty
For going to my family for help
I always have you
To let me know that you are worse off
By helping me
Fine
Then you let me know you're not worried
By helping me
Do you enjoy torturing me
The way I torture myself?
Let me know
Because if you do
Then I'll stay out of your way
For life

SOME SORT OF GENTLE

I turned on the radio
This evening
And I heard a snake speaking
Saying, "If you don't vote for me
Then you will be worse off
Than if you voted for Satan."
I laughed out loud
Knowing that the election
Is going the wrong right way
Again
When will it end
Maybe next spring
After the snow is gone
Though I doubt it
Venom hot enough
To make the north pole melt
I turned on the radio
And the completion
Was incomplete
And I dreamt
That we started all over
And that their left won
So that some sort of gentle
Came through
But I know
It was won months ago
By the less generous side

#1239

MY SORROWS

I walked into the bar
You worked at
And ordered
10 tequila shooters
Even though I don't drink
I put the money
In your cleavage
A one hundred dollar bill
"Keep the change."
I said
I was trying to impress you
It didn't work
You pulled out your pen knife
And cut off all of my fingers
So I couldn't write, paint or take pictures
I couldn't even hold a book
To read
That's what happens
Whenever I try to impress
Someone of the opposite sex
It always backfires
Just like the last time
Now I am missing my left leg
Commiserate
Yeah right
The last time that happened
Was back in the eighties
When I was a teenager
And even then
The girl stood me up
One day later
As to the present
With the shooters
And no fingers

And you being super pissed at me
I couldn't even drown
My sorrows
I don't want to live
This way
But I do anyways
Because a leopard
Doesn't lose its spots
These are the dog days of summer
Because I just made up
All of this
I never try to impress anyone
But myself
But you are still pissed at me
And I am still missing
My fingers
And still trying to drown
My sorrows

THIS LANGUAGE

I am under its thumb
It is a noose
Around my neck
It is a faulty microwave
That corrupts the food I eat
Until it rots out my stomach
This language
I have created
Without any success
Continues to drag me down
As long as I produce it
With no gains
I am slowly killing myself
With no gains in sight
I am dying a slow painful death
With an end coming
To disappoint all who compliment me
I won't go down swinging
I think
I think I should quit
Quit now
Because I see/saw no peak
Quit now
And play chess like Duchamp
Crawl away without swinging
But being crushed by the weight of its thumb
Swinging in the noose
That this language
Tries to contain

LIKE RALPH

I wrote this
The day Johnny Ramone died
The cause was prostate cancer
For his death
Not why I wrote this
Though some would debate that
When an icon dies
It is a crying shame
When a shithead, redneck politician
Like Ralph Klein
Gets to live another second
It is a crying shame
I would like to go to Ralph's home
And tie him up in a chair
Beat him senseless
Douse him in gasoline
Make him watch me...
Maybe shoot his wife
In the back of her head
Then I would like to set him on fire
Woo Hoo! It's a fuckin' pork roast!
But I would have to run away quickly
Not because I am scared
Of getting caught
But because his house
Will explode
From all of his toxic thoughts
Johnny Ramone collected baseball memorabilia
Ralph klein alienated
Myself and my friends
Johnny Ramone made a lot of people
Happy
And for this he died of prostate cancer
Ralph Klein and his ego are way out of hand

So I would like to take matters
Into my own hands
And make sure
He won't be able to alienate
Gays, Chileans, artists,
Homeless, mentally ill, etc., etc.
Johnny Ramone died without a regret
Ralph Klein will hopefully regret
All he has done
For that is why
I would like to end his reign
Johnny's will live on
With everyone of his power chords
He ever played
Long live the Ramones
Painfully slow death to Ralph Klein

MOVING TARGET

You can't defang me
I'll still write about
Murder, torture and death
Only I can defang myself
Slow down myself
Censure myself
Push myself
Stop myself
I will never stop myself
I will always stop myself
From stopping myself
From slowing down
From censorship
I will continue to push myself
To push you
Until you accept me
As a human being
With feelings and rights
I will make you
Think twice about me
And you
And then my job will be complete
And then it will be
On to the next person
You can't defang me
You can try
But you will always fail
Because I am always moving
And you are always still
You'll never hit me
Because I am a moving target
And your aim
Is always off
You should go after

Nazis or the K.K.K.
Not a pussycat like me
You'll never defang me
I
Just
Will
Not
Let
You
Get
Any
Satisfaction
You'll never defang me

#1243

SOMEONE ELSE, SOMEWHERE ELSE

In the end
Have a party
To commemorate
How no longer you hurt
From me and my pain

I shot him down
And hoped that
If there was a heaven
That I would be rejected
Once again
By someone else
Somewhere else
And it would just prove
That rejection
Is my calling
Not my work

In my end
Have a party
To commemorate
How no longer I hurt
From you and your pain

THE LOST ONE

Everything that was lost
Will be found
Will be found once and for all
Time
Money
Lovers
Everything
Will be found
Maybe not the same
But close enough
To make it count for you
Once and for all
And it will all
Put a smile on your face
That won't be lifted
Until you are the one
That is lost
And roles are reversed
And you are the lost one
And someone waits
To find you
Once and for all
Once and for all

PRESS ON

The press got it all wrong
As usual
Oh well....
A few less people to deal with
A few less twisters
Twisters of the truth
I am held captive now
By my silent phone
I stopped calling her
Minutes ago
Because she kept on calling me
"Hon" and "friend"
When I don't even know her last name
I want to break into the nearest mansion
And hide out in the basement
Until my life force
All spills....finally from my parched lips
That were just waiting
For some bread and water
No one who lives at the mansion
Will find me
Until my smell
From my decaying body
Is reported in the press
Again
And I am left trying to defend
My rotting corpse
Again

YOU'VE DONE THIS BEFORE

It's a war of words
It's a word of wars
It's an answer
To your cheetah or leopard
That won't change its spots
You wouldn't stay for company
Just go for broke
And show all
And leave in a flash
You could have taken a load off
I wouldn't have minded
One bit
I want to get closer to you
Maybe you are too young for me
And I won't be able to keep up
With you
Even if you put your load on me
To quote "The Band"
It still feels like a war
When I call you
And that makes me sad
But everybody everywhere
Makes me sad eventually
Even myself
Your words sometimes make me
Sad
Hot and bothered
Laugh
But mostly keep my distance
And that's why
It's a war of words
It's a word of wars
Like you've done this before
And I am just another heart to break

IT HAPPENS A LOT LATELY

This time
I couldn't pull the trigger
And it got me blown to pieces
In the middle
Of a wonderfully orange fall
Colors warm
Temperatures cool enough
To make you wear a sweater
And your cheeks and nose go rosy
There is so much around
But none looking this way
Maybe that's why I couldn't pull the trigger
I couldn't kill an innocent
And it got me blown to pieces
On her bedroom floor
Underneath her just dropped
Pants and underwear
I would rather be in her bed
By myself for a little while
Then with her for a lot
Longer
But at least I get her smell
On her floor
Underneath her pants and underwear
Is it
"Nice guys don't get laid?"
Or
"Nice guys don't get paid?"
Or both?
Or neither?
Or both in good time?
Or neither?
Or whenever it feels right
For the guy?

I know for a fact
That at night
When I am sleeping
I can dream of the future
I just don't remember
The future
Until moments before
The future becomes now
But this has no effect
On this piece of writing
Because it is not a love poem
It is an almost love poem
Which seems to happen a lot lately
I have been told that my eyes' shade of blue
Are hidden behind my glasses
I guess that's a shame
But I need my glasses
To write, read, paint and take photographs
So I wear these frames
Wondering if my eyes
Could be as blue as your's
Or if your's are framed too
By your black and red make up
And your youth
Maybe that is what gets me this way
Yes
I'll blame it on your youth
When I was drinking heavily
To hide my early teenage embarrassment
You were barely out of the womb
Look at Leonard Cohen
He was seeing a thirty year old
When he was fifty five
And he would probably tell me
That the reason he does it
Is because he can
Or maybe I am being cynical
Watching the leaves fall

Outside my lonely bedroom window
Or maybe I am being cynical
About her age, my age or both
Or maybe I am
Trying to hide my thirty something
Embarrassment
At not being able to pull the trigger

#1248

EARLIER AND LATER

Year by year
The losses mount
And the fans go away
And stay away
So I will ask you
What's love got to do
With this mess?
It's not exactly clear
But I look around anyways
And all I see
Is a group broke
Broke and broken dreams
Broken hearts
Broken spirits
Broken
Just broke and broken
It's times like this
I feel so lost and helpless
The sun is setting
Earlier and earlier
The sun is rising
Later and later
I never felt like
I had everything going for me
Maybe that's why I have
These few friends
I read the bible yesterday
And I felt alienated
All over again
Again
And again
If life is a game
Some days I just want to forfeit
And move on

Somewhere else
And hope that I won't need
Overtime again
To get on a winning streak
So would I know
A winning streak
If I was on one?
Ahhh....
That is the multi-million dollar question
Would I know one
If I was on one?
When I am broke and broken
And there is less
Sun to work with
Everyday
If life is a game
Does everyone win eventually?
Another multi-million dollar question
Anymore and the contract
Will be torn up
And I will be left
Broke and broken
With the broke and broken

#1249

In the battle
In my skull
The voices, sights
More sounds and smells
I am left wondering
If what's real is real
And if I am a humanitarian
If I can't even get my own shit
Together
I listen, see, smell, taste
A lot
And I am not sure
If the battle in my skull
Makes a fake or
Makes it real
My shoes are made in China
Does that make them
More real
Than if they were made here
Maybe I shouldn't complain so much
About stuff like this or that
And move on
But in the heat of the battle
I feel as if no one wins
When I am so lonely
That I call you everyday
You politely put up
With my shit
So I run with it
And hope that I don't piss you off
This battle
This battle in my skull
Makes me stray
Be nice to me
And now I stay
Or come back

Time and time
And time again
And again
I got "hope" tattooed on me
So that I will never lose it
And that my final hope
Hope that the battle ceases
And that you can handle me
And my eccentricities
Now
Look
There's the sunrise
Let's walk into it together
And
Now
Look
There's the sunset
Let's walk into it together to
And be as one
So I won't have to worry anymore
That my battle claims you
Another victim of my importation
Of a sweat factory worker's shit
Let's move here together
As one
With the battle being over
And neither of us its victims

UNDERSTAND

Understand
Where the rats in the sewer
Come from
They came from what we built
Out of our darkest recesses
Of our mind's leprosy
The rats chew at the floor
Underneath our carpet
Until they poke their noses
Tentatively in the stale air
Of our white trash homes
Come on and watch them
Duke it out with the black widows
And scorpions hiding
Underneath our show
And piles of unwashed clothing
You think I don't know?
Oh, I know
How strong we have to be
To burn this shit into oblivion
You can pound your bible
All you want
It won't hide the darkness
The rapists
The murderers
The terrorists
The drunks and junkies
Who all lost their sweet side
When they understood
Where all the rats came from
Understand
Where all the rats came from

#1251

EVERYTHING WAS WRONG

When I am being followed
I slow down
And let the follower pass
Or mug me
Or both
And then I carry on
As if nothing happened
I know my rights
I know how to defend myself
Even if it means one of our deaths
To quote Henry Miller
"I am not afraid of death,
I am afraid of dying."
That's where I stand too
Don't get me wrong
I am not afraid of living either

I remember one time
With my girlfriend
In a movie theatre
1 girl and 3 guys
Were making a bunch of noise
During the movie
I stood up
And yelled at them
To, "Shut the fuck up!"
And called them
The stupidest motherfuckers on earth
Everyone in the theatre clapped

After the movie
My girlfriend and I were being followed
Out of the theatre
And onto the street

I told my girlfriend to keep walking
I turned around
And the three guys
Were standing there
I asked them,
"What are you going to do?"
And turned around
And walked slowly
To my girlfriend
They wouldn't have done shit
Because of all the people watching
I am so sick of angry young men
No, boys
Who get drunk
And do stupid shit
I would like to take them all
To the nearest landfill
And bury them alive
There
Are you boys happy?
I have now forgotten
How this started
And what the point of this is?
And how to end this
I don't know
Maybe I like the danger
Of trying to end something
That was started by someone else

#1252

BETWEEN US

Listen
Listening
To what is now noise
Hoping
It will be music
To dance to
To love to
To love
To be dragged
Through the streets
Of Paris
Dead from Syphilis
O.K.
Now I have lost all control
And I am rambling
About shit
That I don't know about
But that I can only speculate about
Music
Is the only thing I have in common
With some people
I hope that there is more
Between us
But I am not sure
We talk so little
And I am afraid
To go further
Unless you give me permission
This waiting
Is like Chinese water torture
It goes on and on and on
And on
So now it is music
Not noise

And I will hope that it will pass time
Better than if it was Chinese water torture
But with all this waiting
It may as well be
Chinese water torture

MY WORK WORK

While the white walls go up
I wish that they were meaningless
But wishing that wish is wishful thinking
It is not funny anymore
How I go about making my work work
Sometimes
Not always
It is at the expense of others
My latest is not at the expense of anyone
But myself and my wasting of time
Oh, how I waste time
Thinking of you
Hoping that you will not pass up
The opportunity of having me
Even if it is only for once
I know it will probably be never
If I can taste it
That's the way it goes
When the white walls go up
And I go down on you
Just to make my work work

#1254

WHERE WOULD I BE WITH YOU

I think about you
And I know I screwed up
And I know you would agree and think
That I am a screw up
That I can't do anything right
That I am always relying
On family and friends
To bail me out
But you don't know
That it makes me want
To jump in front of a train
Or the promise of falling
Off of a tall bridge
Overdosing on medication
Cutting my wrists open
Paying back my debts
And then dropping off the face
Of the earth
O.K.
You don't believe me
So prove me wrong
Show me that I will have
A life worth living
Immediately!
But you can't
You just stand back
With a sneer on your face
Not caring that it makes me want
To die
I think about you
And realize
The pointlessness of it all
And try to sleep
This all off

And hope that when I wake
I will prove you wrong
Or
Not wake up at all

#1255

THE LAST WAR

I feel like it will never happen
Everybody on the whole earth
Rallying behind one cause
The last war
The people in the last war
Will wonder what they are fighting for
When everyone around them are not fighting
It will,
The war will
Stop out of embarrassment
Of how badly outnumbered
The fighters are
And that will be the last war
Christians, Jews, Atheists, Agnostics, Buddhists,
Muslims, etc., etc., etc.
Black, white, yellow, red, etc., etc., etc.
Gay, straight, bi, etc., etc., etc.
Will all get along
They realize that we are all people
Who deserve to be loved
Not hated
And war will just end
But I still feel
Like it will never happen
That the world will explode
Before we all get along
I am so sad
And you are so mad
How can war end
When we exploit others differences
Instead of embracing them
I still feel like it will never happen

#1256

THIS DESPERATION

This desperation is here
Here to stay it seems
I wish I was more
More like a machine
Then my bad luck of late
Wouldn't hurt me as much
If at all
I sleep too much
I exercise too little
And now I am paying for it
As I get older
Nothing to live for
But my work
Nothing to die for
But my work
Maybe I had my one chance
And passed it up
By mistake
I just know
I wouldn't pass it up
On purpose
I have to do anything
To get out of this mess
So I just know
It had to be a mistake
It had to be a mistake
Because now
This desperation is here
And I never wanted it this way

#1257

FLY PAN AM

Just got home
From seeing three great bands
Now I am home alone
Flat lining
In the quiet of my apartment
I wish
You were here with me
But that's O.K.
I will get by
On my own
I've done it before
I'll do it again

LAST NIGHT'S DREAMS

I had a dream last night
About Sharon and Ozzy Osbourne
Sharon had just had a baby
And was looking at it and smiling
She looked at Ozzy and said
"We should be able to do something
With this, shouldn't we?"
Ozzy smiled and nodded
Ozzy nodded and smiled

I had a dream last night
In it, I was carrying your tiny body
Down a hill into a field
I said to you that,
"Something terrible will happen
At ten to three pm."
You agreed and put your head
In the nape of my neck
And I felt your breath on that spring day

These dreams disturbed me
Because I am a big fan
Of the Osbournes
And you and your tiny body
They haunt me
Well into the afternoon
So much so
I hope that when I went to sleep tonight
That it would be more peaceful

LITTLE ONES

It's like New Year's day
It may snow a little
But nothing really changes
It's like talking to them
They've got their good paying jobs
Or their pensions
And their houses and cars and pets
And don't forget their friends
Who make me uncomfortable
Who I make uncomfortable
My work is to be kept
In the basement pantry
Cool and dark
Their's proudly displayed
In the brightest room
And I am not supposed to be bitter?
So I get home
And see that there is a message
In my voice mail box
I hope that it is you little one
But deep down inside
I know it won't be
Do you have these problems too?
If so,
Can we talk about it sometime
Over a snack in a quiet cafe?
Maybe we will have something
In common
I could vent
You could vent
And we could get along
Gloriously
And you could come to mine
And I yours

And we could laugh together
How silly they are
With all of their stuff and snot
And how perfect we are
With our disheveled clothes
And broken dreams
But it's like New Year's day
And I am home alone
With an empty home
And an empty feeling
That only goes away
Only when I think of you
So I will go to sleep
Thinking of how
I don't fit in with them
And how I would like to be
With you and hope that together
We will have some sort of
Diplomatic immunity
From them and their stuff and snot

WRETCH

I should keep my mouth shut
About my family
They try their best around me
They have never murdered me
I have murdered them
They are not a time bomb
I am
I am so disrespectful to them
In my world
You would think that my family
Were Hitler's family
They try to help me out
As much as they can
And I am an ungrateful wretch

Without them
I
Am
Nothing
When will I show some respect?
When the pie is globalized?
Blood from a stone
Blood from a family
Blood from a stone
Respect

#1261

HAZY, HOLIDAY MONDAY

How come you do this to me
With your eyes of coal
And your heart of stone
And your blood of vinegar
You tear at me
As if I were your last meal
And your timing is impeccable
You never call me
Unless there is a problem
Or are you hungry for my powerlessness?
On this Monday of thanks
It's something else that I don't get
Something about you
And something about this holiday
I feel hungover when you call
And you sense it
And use it to your advantage
And you roast me alive
And I will ask you again
How come you do this to me
I am powerless to stop me
Now I know
This holiday is not a holiday
It is my funeral
Thanks to you

ANOTHER ONE

I feel another debt coming on
Yup, there it is
But maybe my luck will change
I know why you see him
He is better looking and more fun probably
I am poor
I am poor
I am poor
And tired
All of the time feel like
You see all of my faults
And none of his
So how can I compete
So you laugh at me
When I am not around
So I go out
And spend money I don't have
And get into more and more debt
Bigger and bigger
Yup, there it is
Another one in money
And another one in emotions

MADE TO BE

I promise
Not
To write about you again

It's only skin deep
But it's deep enough for me
Your black hair
Dyed I'm sure
Your blue eyes
All natural because you told me
And you never lie
Your breasts
Your flat belly
Showing off your tattoos
On your pelvis
Your hips
Your ass
Your legs
All of it
Is only skin deep
I know I am not in style
And you are
I still can't get enough of you
Of you
Of you
More of you
Less of me
You've got me so bad
But it's only skin deep

Promises are
Made to be
Broken

#1264

TREADING IN APATHY

It's like what
Bob Dylan said
I'm feeling like a stranger
Nobody sees
Maybe that's why
I am so shy
But the birds are still
Singing
Whether I like it
Or not
And when someone is
Drinking and driving
And also says
That they are dead
Then you know that they aren't
And should be shot
In the head
Before they do some real damage
Now I am 32 miles from nowhere
And 13 from hell
For all the things
I've said so well
If I've kicked you
In the ass
Good
Because you can tread only
For so long
Before you either drown
Or swim
Because something's got to change

#1266

DAY JOB, NIGHT JOB

Sink before this reason
It is the job of the artist
To be honest with only themselves
Then everything else will fall
Into place
The second job of the artist
Is to police themselves
Not others
Contrary to popular belief
If someone is fucked up enough
To do something
After listening, seeing or reading
Something an artist has created
No matter how reprehensible
By the artist
No matter how reprehensible
By the viewer, listener, etc.
Then they were fucked up enough
That they were going to do it anyways
In a matter of time
Police be the police
Viewer be the viewer
And artist be the artist
Don't blame the artist
For someone's fuck up
That someone has to take
Full responsibility for their actions
And as for the artist
They need only take responsibility
For their quality of work
This has been said before
By people more intelligent than me
But you still don't listen
But you still don't

Sink before this reason

THE SHOOT

I'll bring the car
You bring the guns
I'll drive
And you shoot
Take a picture
Any time you want
I don't care
We won't get caught
Ever
Because we never said
Goodbye or even hello
My poor driving skills
Won't even get us caught
Because your aim is impeccable
Shoot
Anything that moves
Shoot
Anything that doesn't move
Just get the shot

We've been going at this
For hours now
Leaving a trail
In our wake
This is awesome
This was awesome
We'll have to do it again
Sometime soon, hopefully
Burroughs would be proud

THE NEWEST OF THE NEW

I can't stand what's on the radio

Anymore

Girl good, boy bad

So you're tired of seeing

Women get cut up in daily life

Well, not all men do that

Well, maybe you should stop it yourself

Sometimes

You are your own worst enemy

Enemy of you

Enemy of me

Enemy of the state

Enemy of the world

I say what's inside

I put it out to discuss

Not with me

With the guilty parties

I am not a guilty party

At least I don't feel that way

And yes

I get to sleep just fine

So I can't stand what's on the T.V.

So I turn it off

And I get to sleep

Just fine

Just fine

IRRATIONAL

I shoveled snow this morning

A little while later

The sky broke open

And let loose more white flakes

Big and fluffy

Sensitive to my warm skin

One flake landed on my top right eyelashes

It took awhile

But eventually it melted

Into a tear

One single tear

That ran down my cheek

I wiped it with the back of my hand

And went inside

Trying not to match

This fake tear

With a real one

#1270

EXTRA SHIFT

Yesterday
I lost sight of the sky
And forgot how to dream
Of hope for a future
A positive future
Maybe it is just denial
And it is right in front
Of my nose
But getting a grip on it
Is like trying to hug
A greased pig
It's just bitter resentment
I think it is anyways
You tried to bring me down
A notch
Only I can do that
A weakling like yourself
Can't come even close
To accomplishing that
Only a weakling like myself can
I realized all of this
Yesterday

THE WRONG ANSWER

She asked me
Who I wrote for
My answer
(Which has never changed)
Myself
Was the wrong answer
She stopped talking to me
So I went home
And fell asleep
With my clothes on
On my bed
Later I got up
And listened to melancholy music
And cried that I had to sell
More music to make rent
Because I spent too much
The day before
I feel so dumb
That I can't control myself
Financially, emotionally or
With others
Now I realize
Why I want to die
All of the time
But I keep it inside
Hoping that I don't overflow
And end up dead
In my clothes
On my bed
Because I am sure that this answer
Is the wrong one too

#1272

I hope that I see you again
And we can become friends
And then maybe more
I hope that I don't intimidate you
The way you intimidate me
I hope that we can laugh with each other
Not at each other
Or if we do laugh at each other
It's the way friends do
Can we become friends?
I hope that I see you again

#1273

PRIVATE NAME

It's the call at the end of the day
The one that I slept through
The phone ringing
I didn't recognize the number
On my call display
Maybe it was "The Call"
The one that would save me
But it just said "Private"
And I am left wondering
Who is that private
That they can't leave a message

#1274

TRY IT

You should follow my lead
And write more people off
It leads to a purer lifestyle
And sometimes when you find
That special someone
It is even more special
Because you have starved yourself
Of all that waste that's out there
Try it
And maybe you'll end up married
Or torn apart with grief
Because someone else will let you down
And you will hit the floor hard
Try it
And maybe you'll hate this place
Like I do
And I will teach you to swim
Instead of teaching you to drown

UNDER APPRECIATED

Are you happy
That I am dead inside
Are you happy
That what comes out
Is always the falling
Or the fallen
Will you tell me
What time it is
When I am back
With the living
The last group shot
I was in
I wasn't really
I was off to the side
And all my sisters and cousins
Were scrunched together
Like they were trying to keep warm
And I was off to the side
Easy to Photoshop out
When the outside
Matches the inside

#1276

IN TIMES

In times like our's
It seems like being a volunteer
Is never enough
I don't mind not getting paid
As long as I like the job
If I am getting paid
It had better be near perfect
Or else I have to come to the realization
It would be time to move on
My volunteer position is great
Relaxing, no stress
All the jobs I have had
Are just the opposite
If only I got paid
For the jobs I liked
I would be a happier person
In times like these

#1277

OUR FALL TOGETHER

It's been awhile
But I remembered
When we played pool
All morning
Then going out for breakfast
At a diner that no longer exists
I remembered
Just the other day
A bus ride back home from my parent's place
Where we felt each other up
The whole ride home
We could hardly wait to get home
So we could have sex
I even remembered
Lying around naked
All day on your birthday
Watching movies
It's been awhile
Since I thought about shit like this
It seems that the fall season
Brings the most change
Oranges, yellows on the ground
And in the trees
Sometimes the early white
The change in the environment
Makes me think of you
And starting school
And baseball playoffs
And a new hockey season
And our fall together
When nothing went wrong
Until the new year
And all the shit hit the fan
New year

New you and I from us
New you
New I
No more us
Funny
I would have thought change
Would have come in the dying season
Not the dead season
But maybe the dead season
Killed the "me"
In "you"

#1278

I listened to your favorite artist tonight
In the hope of you hearing my loneliness
And you would give me a phone call
It didn't work
So I turned off my stereo for the night
And had my usual drug overdose for the night

REASONABLE RESPONSES TO AN UNREASONABLE GAME

A few nights ago
I was watching the stars
And one star
Above a chimney
On a small house
Across the street
Flickered
And then died
It was a warm fall evening
The kind that made you feel
That snow wouldn't be coming for awhile yet
Nothing
Was coming out of the chimney
To obscure my view
I watched intently
For nights on end
And
No
Star
On the night I gave up
I met this black girl
And her and I
Went out for tea
I hadn't noticed
Her little pot belly
But she pointed it out
Saying she didn't know
Who the father was
I felt bad for her
And told her so
She told me not to worry about it
Because she wasn't
Silence
Then I told her about the missing star

She told me not to worry about it
But I told her I would
Because of all of the life
That was snuffed out
Silence
Then she called me a pussy
I called her a bitch
And I got up to leave
And she called me
A sexist, racist
But the door closed on the rest
And I went to the nearest liquor store
And I bought one of those boxes of wine
And went home
I called up this girl I knew
And she came over
And we both got really drunk
Then she tried to give me head
When she knew damn well
I didn't like that sort of thing
She called me a pussy
(Second time in less than a day)
And punched me in my pot belly
And left
Left me with the wine
And my pants and underwear
Around my knees
I didn't even get to tell her
About the missing star
So I watched you
In your newly made home
A few houses down
From the little one
With the chimney
You sat at your computer all night
When you turned out the lights
Turned out the lights
Turned off the computer

I still couldn't tell
What gender you were
Doesn't matter I guess
I won't be able to meet anyone
In the condition I am in
So I passed out
In my door way
With the door unlocked
But closed
So if anyone tried to get in
To my compartment
The door would ram against me
I woke up days later
After the world series curse ended
I missed it all
Even when the head girl
Left a dozen or so messages
On my phone's answering machine
But I didn't have much time
Because I had a hangover to cure
And messages to erase
And the police to deal with
Because they were smashing
My compartment's door against me
Telling me to clean myself up
And to get a fucking job
I told them, O.K., O.K., O.K.
Slammed the door shut
Locked it
And went and had a long hot shower
Got out
Got dressed
Got out
Realized that it was midday
And I couldn't see any stars
And in the irrational state I was
Thought that all the stars had died
And that I would have to create

My own star or stars

To replace the dead ones

Because stars die all of the time

Sucking life with them

And eventually my star would die too

And someone else

Somewhere else

Will notice it

And open up

And create their own star or stars to replace

The ones that are lost

#1280

ALREADY

Can you bring me some words
And help me back up again
Or is it all in my head
Already
The climate grew cold
And no one seemed to notice
That people were dropping like flies
Does that make me better
For noticing the people falling
And everyone else worse
For not noticing
Hey
I barely noticed
That I was one of the fallen
Who needs a hand to get up
It's all a source of drama
It's all a reality show gone sour
If that's possible
I am too scared to ask for a hand
Because I am scared
That I'll drag you down with me
And the rest of the flies
I don't want to be responsible
For anyone but myself most times
Hey
Look at this
Look at all of the words
That I brought up
Maybe I don't need your hand
After all
Maybe it's all in my head
Already

MOSQUITOES

I had hoped to see you again
But it is not looking too promising
It has been a month or so
And nothing
No sign of you
What is left to write
When I constantly meet beautiful people
Who constantly flit out of my life
Like a mosquito
That has got its fill
Except
The beautiful people
Shouldn't be compared to insects
Of any sort
I just couldn't find a better simile
But the flitting beautiful people
All take a little from me
I give
And give
And give
And nothing
I guess I shouldn't put so much faith
In people
But
I still hope to see you again

#1282

IT IS

My writing
Is only catastrophic music
It should heal me
And enlighten the few
Who read it
My writing
Is just a newborn
With a heart defect
That surgery can't fix
Healing
Enlightening
Whichever it is
Is not "only" or "just"
It "is"

MAYBE IT WAS THAT TIME OF THE MONTH?

When I first met you

I thought that you were a cliche

Dyke

You know the type

The kind with short hair

The kind with horn rimmed glasses and an attitude problem

But I quickly found out

You weren't a dyke

Because you were seeing

The snottiest guy in town

But the rest of the cliches were true

You like to think

That you're oh so open minded

But you're oh so the opposite

An insensitive brat

Who never did any research

Into my illness

So you had no right

To pass judgement

But pass you did

With lots of venom

And lots of mixed signals

You are the type of woman

Who makes me mistrust all women

I come in contact with

#1284

I have got to hurry
Because the hottest hits
The biggest flicks
And the brightest stars
Are all coming to kill me
Before I come all over
This page again

GREETINGS

We walked towards each other
After ten months of no talking
In a 3 month span I called you 4 times
Leaving my number everytime
Nothing
And now you are smiling
And touching my arm
Expecting me to acknowledge you
You were never around
When I needed a friend
And you expect it to be the same
Go fuck yourself
I hope that you are stupid enough
To call me
So I can give you a piece of my mind
Child

FAMILY TIES

I dreamt
That we all still lived together
The two of you
Were still harassing me
But now I was fighting back
And it made everything worse
Our mother sympathized with me
Because I was going back to high school
And Dad had just released
All of my snakes
From their bag
By accident
So I was furious
Pushing tables into the two of you
And such
Basically being irrational
Some would say
As usual
And my dreams are so screwed up
As usual
My dreams aren't sugarcubes
Melting on your tongue
As usual
What I dreamt
Is close to what was reality
As usual
As usual

CUT MY LOSSES

It would be nice
But I can't bank on it
Because she is lousy
With dates
And I am not
She is so young and pretty
And I am not
She said
She would do that favor
And then balks
Everytime I call
Anything for my work eh?
Well
Almost anything
Everything except humiliating myself
Everytime I call
It would be nice
But I can't bank on it
I just have to learn
When to cut my losses

NEVER SAY NEVER

In the early hours

I dream of meeting my heroes

But deep down inside

I know that I never will

I stumble through obscurity

Trying to pay my bills

Barely getting by

Thinking of all of the "yous"

I have written about from afar

Or have passed on through

My life

Leaving scars across my stomach

And arms

And legs

And chest

And I know how much farther

I have to get noticed

And I am scared once again

About failure

About bankruptcy

About obscurity

And I know that I should

Never say never

As well as

Being careful what you wish for

This all happens

In the early hours

When I am weak and powerless

#1289

TO THIS DAY

It's so slick

I keep turning around

To make sure it's still there

This disease that haunts me

So far I am calm

So far I am cool

So far I am collected

There is no way to promote it

Until I am getting away with murder

Whether or not you like it or not

I will continue on

Trying to make my and my friend's and my family's

Worlds a better place

Eventually it will spread

Because it is so slick

And to this day

My first name may be "misery"

But my last is "strength"

#1290

BURIED IN DEATH

I refuse to get buried

By you and your ignorance

You are not even breathing anymore

But you still insist

On acting like we are friends

When you never even paid me

For the grief you caused me

Your last touch on me

Pains me

Because it was unexpected

And unwanted by myself

It's like listening to a dead junkie's words

But making sure

You don't get buried by them

There

I said it again

Buried

And it is over now

And I am still standing

And walking

And talking

And creating

And I am not buried

By you and your ignorance

#1291

NEED A WANT

Those songs of happiness
Are just stains on my bed sheets
Just like listening
To the Cure's first twelve albums
Front to back
Back to front
Just because
I am so fucking happy
I need something good
I need some good luck
I need some luck
I need a lucky charm
I need somebody charming
I need
I need
I need
A want
I want
I want
I want
I want more pain
Because there's not enough
To go around anyways
What good is your open hand
When you can't back up
Your openness
With strength
Because you have none
When the sky opens up
And bleeds
More shit on you
What do they always say?
If it wasn't for bad luck
We wouldn't have any

Those stains on my bed sheets
Are now gone
Because I did my laundry
And now all I have left
Are my Cure records
And clean sheets

#1292

LAUGHING AT YOU FALLING

Stop me

If you've heard this one before

Sometimes

I just can't stop myself

Sometimes

I just can't control myself

So let's just get to it

So let's just get it on

And move on

Because I think I need a hug

And then I will be on my way

Because I think I know

You won't be following me

Anytime soon

And you won't be leading me

Anytime soon either

So get the fuck out of the way

And let me move

On down the line

I offered my conversation

And you scowled at me and went across the room

To sit by yourself

Whenever I try to be friendly

Someone

Somewhere

At sometime

Shits on me

Stupid bitch

You'll get your's

At sometime

Somewhere

By someone

And then you'll regret

Your ignorance

And I'll be around the corner
Laughing
At
You
Falling

#1293

After the night was over
When you touched
My left arm
And when I got home
I had to make sure
There were no marks left
To blend in with my tattoos and scars
Nothing
Tell all of your friends
I would rather
Roll around naked
In hundreds of razor blades
Than feel your touch again

THE ENDING

Listening to early Sonic Youth
"Bad Moon Rising"
All scratchy from listening to it
Far too many times
It is good ending music
It is good starting over music
So I started to hit it
Knowing full well
That it should be over
Knowing full well
That the next page
Will start all over again
And no one can stop me
You can charge me with assault
You can torture me for days on end
You can ban my books
You can burn my books
But I will still get paid
And I will still be able to live
Off of this shit
Eventually
And by the time you have discovered
Me and my work
It will be too late to stop me
Even if it is the end
Even if it is the end
You
Will
Never
Stop
Me

www.ingramcontent.com/pod-product-compliance
Lightning Source LLC
Chambersburg PA
CBHW050554300426
44112CB00013B/1918